Donated by
Jacquelyn C. Miller
In Loving Memory of Her
Husband, Bruce.

TEAM SPIRIT®

SMART BOOKS FOR YOUNG FANS

THE TAMPA BAY RAYS

BY

MARK STEWART

NORWOODHOUSE PRESS

CHICAGO, ILLINOIS

Norwood House Press
P.O. Box 316598
Chicago, Illinois 60631

For information regarding Norwood House Press, please visit our website at:
www.norwoodhousepress.com or call 866-565-2900.

All photos courtesy of Getty Images except the following:
Black Book Partners Archives (7, 9, 10, 17, 18, 19, 22, 23, 24, 25, 35 bottom, 36, 37, 38, 39, 41, 42 bottom),
SportsChrome (8), Tom DiPace (14, 16, 27, 35 top),
Topps, Inc. (15, 21, 29, 34 top, 40, 42 top, 43 top, 45),
Author's Collection (33), Matt Richman (48).
Cover Photo: J. Meric/Getty Images

The memorabilia and artifacts pictured in this book are presented for educational and informational purposes,
and come from the collection of the author.

Editor: Mike Kennedy
Designer: Ron Jaffe
Project Management: Black Book Partners, LLC.
Special thanks to Topps, Inc.

Library of Congress Cataloging-in-Publication Data

Stewart, Mark, 1960-
  The Tampa Bay Rays / by Mark Stewart. -- Library ed.
    p. cm. -- (Team spirit)
  Includes bibliographical references and index.
  Summary: "A Team Spirit Baseball edition featuring the Tampa Bay Rays that
chronicles the history and accomplishments of the team. Includes access to
the Team Spirit website, which provides additional information, updates and
photos"--Provided by publisher.
  ISBN 978-1-59953-498-5 (library : alk. paper) -- ISBN 978-1-60357-378-8
(ebook) 1. Tampa Bay Rays (Baseball team)--History--Juvenile literature.
I. Title.
  GV875.T26S74 2012
  796.357'640975965--dc23
                                        2011048463

Manufactured in the United States of America in North Mankato, Minnesota.
196N—012012

COVER PHOTO: The Rays celebrate a win on their home field in 2011.

TABLE OF CONTENTS

ABOUT OUR GLOSSARY

In this book, there may be several words that you are reading for the first time. Some are sports words, some are new vocabulary words, and some are familiar words that are used in an unusual way. All of these words are defined on page 46. Throughout the book, sports words appear in **bold type**. Regular vocabulary words appear in ***bold italic type***.

MEET THE RAYS

Sometimes, the difference between winning and losing a baseball game is so small that fans don't even notice it. Is the same true when a team rises from the bottom of the standings? The Tampa Bay Rays turned their luck around almost overnight. At least that is the way it seemed.

The Rays carefully built their team one player at a time over many years. Each hitter and pitcher that the team added had to learn how to work together and win together. When that day finally came, the Rays were the most exciting story in baseball.

This book tells the story of the Rays. For many years, other teams in baseball hardly paid attention to Tampa Bay. Today, everyone keeps an eye on them. As the Rays have proven, with a little patience, it's possible to create a team that wins year after year after year.

Evan Longoria returns to the dugout after a home run. He is one of the players that has helped the Rays become a winning team.

GLORY DAYS

n the spring of 1998, two new teams played their first season in the big leagues. The Arizona Diamondbacks became part of the **National League (NL)**, and the Tampa Bay Devil Rays joined the **American League (AL)**. Tampa Bay is a large body of water on the west coast of Florida. Two of the cities nearby are Tampa and St. Petersburg. The Devil Rays played their games in a domed stadium in St. Petersburg. They shortened their name to Rays in 2008.

The Rays started with players chosen from other teams in a special **draft**. Over the next few years, they added more *veterans*. Some, such as Fred McGriff and Wade Boggs, had grown up in this part of Florida.

They wanted to finish their careers where they started. The Rays also signed Rolando Arrojo and Jose Canseco. Their roots were in Cuba, a country with many connections to Florida. Arrojo became the first Tampa Bay player to be picked for the **All-Star Game**.

At the same time, the Rays were busy training young players in the **minor leagues**. Julio Lugo, Aubrey Huff, Toby Hall, Randy Winn, Rocco Baldelli, and Carl Crawford all played their way into the Tampa Bay lineup. In 2004, the team began to show signs of improvement. The Rays won 12 games in a row during the season and finished in fourth place in the **AL East**.

After the 2004 season, the decision to go with young players became even easier. Tampa Bay soon needed a manager who could build a winner from the pieces the team was assembling. In 2006, the Rays hired Joe Maddon to lead the club. Over the next two seasons, Maddon learned a lot about his players. He saw great talent and a fierce desire to win.

The Rays had a good pitching staff that included James Shields, Matt Garza, Andy Sonnanstine, Scott Kazmir, and Edwin Jackson. The team's top hitters were Crawford, B.J. Upton, Carlos Pena, and Evan Longoria. Nobody worked harder than Longoria or was a better player in the **clutch**. He helped lead the way as Tampa Bay showed signs of becoming a championship *contender*.

In 2008, the Rays enjoyed their first winning season. They went from last place in the AL East the year before all the way to the **World Series**. No one had expected Tampa Bay to win the **pennant**. Even so,

LEFT: Evan Longoria is a star who is not afraid to play hard and get his uniform dirty.   **ABOVE**: Joe Maddon shouts encouragement to his team.

it was disappointing when the Rays did not capture the championship. Still, the players gained tremendous confidence and experience.

Since their great 2008 season, the Rays have worked very hard to make it back to the World Series. They returned to the **playoffs** in 2010 and 2011. Both years, Tampa Bay was beaten by the Texas Rangers.

The Rays remain focused on their goal. They prefer to build around the players that the team has developed in the minors. Exciting young stars such as David Price,

Jeremy Hellickson, Matt Moore, and Desmond Jennings all joined Tampa Bay at around the same time. They have learned to play smart, unselfish baseball. That's the kind of attitude that Rays fans hope will bring a World Series championship to Tampa Bay.

LEFT: David Price fires a fastball toward home plate.
ABOVE: Jeremy Hellickson won 13 games in 2011.

HOME TURF

The Rays play in a domed stadium that was built in 1990. The stadium was built with the hope that the Chicago White Sox would move there. When that did not happen, the Tampa Bay Lightning hockey team moved in. After the Rays arrived in 1998, the stadium was *remodeled* to feel more like an old-time ballpark. Some day, the team would like to open a new stadium near the waterfront in downtown St. Petersburg.

One of the unusual things about the Rays' stadium are the walkways that hang from the ceiling. High fly balls that hit these "catwalks" are in play. In a 2006 game, Jonny Gomes belted a ball that landed on a catwalk and slowly rolled off. Gomes had already touched third base and was headed home when the shortstop caught the ball. The umpire called Gomes out.

BY THE NUMBERS

- The Rays' stadium has 34,078 seats.
- The distance from home plate to the left field foul pole is 315 feet.
- The distance from home plate to the center field fence is 404 feet.
- The distance from home plate to the right field foul pole is 322 feet.

The lighted catwalks can be seen at the top of the Rays' stadium.

F or their first 10 seasons, the Rays used green and black as their main team colors. Their caps had the letters *TB*, which stands for Tampa Bay. They also showed a swimming manta ray (also called a devil ray). Their jerseys said either *Tampa Bay* or *Devil Rays* across the front.

When Tampa Bay switched its name to Rays, the change was made on the team's uniforms, too. It was the first time in more than 40 years that a team took a new name without moving to another city. The Houston Colt .45s did the same thing in 1965 when they became the Astros.

Tampa Bay's uniforms are more colorful today. The team replaced its familiar green and black with a combination of dark blue, light blue, and gold. The team changed its *logo* to a baseball diamond and a sunburst. For special occasions, the Rays sometimes wear alternate uniforms that include either a dark blue or light blue jersey.

LEFT: Desmond Jennings runs the bases in Tampa Bay's 2011 home uniform.
ABOVE: This 1998 trading card shows Fred McGriff in the team's first road uniform.

WE WON!

Change was the theme in Tampa Bay heading into the 2008 season. The team shortened its name from Devil Rays to Rays. It switched to new team colors, plus updated caps and uniforms. The biggest change, however, came on the field. After 10 years in a row with a losing record, the Rays were looking like winners.

Tampa Bay welcomed plenty of new players, too. Troy Percival became the main relief pitcher for the Rays. Starting pitcher Matt Garza and shortstop Jason Bartlett arrived after a trade with the Minnesota Twins. The most important addition to the Rays was Evan Longoria. He had been a star in college and the minor leagues. Longoria joined the team a few weeks after the season began and took over the starting job at third base.

The Rays played good baseball in the first half of the season. They were in first place in the AL East by the All-Star Game. However, no

one really expected their good fortune to continue. After all, Tampa Bay had finished with the worst record in the AL East the season before. But the Rays weren't relying on luck to win games. Manager Joe Maddon kept his team relaxed and focused. Tampa Bay batters got big hits when the team needed them, and the pitchers learned the value of throwing strikes and attacking opposing hitters.

Everyone on the Tampa Bay roster contributed to the team's success. Maddon had a knack for finding the right player to use in every spot. Scott Kazmir was one of five pitchers that won at least 10 games. When Longoria, Percival, and Carl Crawford were injured, other Rays filled in. The team didn't skip a beat, and the Rays won the AL East by two games over the Boston Red Sox.

Tampa Bay could not have done this without the help of the fans. They filled the Rays' stadium and energized the players with their loud and excited cheers. Not surprisingly, Tampa Bay had the best home record in baseball in 2008.

The Rays kept on winning in the playoffs. First, they defeated the Chicago White Sox. Kazmir, James Shields, and Andy Sonnanstine each got a win on the mound. Outfielder B.J. Upton hit two home runs in the final game.

The Rays then met the Red Sox in the **American League Championship Series (ALCS)**. Even though Boston had finished behind the Rays, most people thought the Red Sox would win because of their experience in the **postseason**. At first, it looked as if Boston was headed back to the World Series. The Rays lost the first game at home. Climbing out of that hole would be difficult. But the Rays bounced back and won the next game in 11 innings, thanks to home runs by Longoria, Upton, and Cliff Floyd.

When the series moved to Boston, Tampa Bay appeared to take control. The Rays won the next two games and had a lead in Game 5. The Red Sox responded with

ABOVE: Justin Upton   **RIGHT**: Matt Garza

a thrilling comeback to win 8–7. The series returned to Tampa with the Rays needing just one victory to advance to the World Series.

Game 6 did not go as planned for the Rays. They grabbed an early lead, but Boston clawed its way back. The Red Sox won 4-2 to force the *decisive* Game 7.

Maddon handed the ball to Garza to start the final game of the series. He

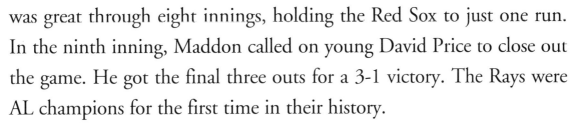

was great through eight innings, holding the Red Sox to just one run. In the ninth inning, Maddon called on young David Price to close out the game. He got the final three outs for a 3-1 victory. The Rays were AL champions for the first time in their history.

All of Florida celebrated Tampa Bay's victory. No one was going to push the Rays around anymore! Unfortunately, they lost in the World Series to the Philadelphia Phillies. But the Rays and their fans were proud. By overcoming the odds, Tampa Bay had given baseball fans all over the country something to cheer about.

GO-TO GUYS

To be a true star in baseball, you need more than a quick bat and a strong arm. You have to be a "go-to guy"—someone the manager wants on the pitcher's mound or in the batter's box when it matters most. Fans of the Rays have had a lot to cheer about over the years, including these great stars …

THE PIONEERS

FRED MCGRIFF   First Baseman

• BORN: 10/31/1963   • PLAYED FOR TEAM: 1998 TO 2001 & 2004

Fred McGriff was Tampa Bay's first star slugger. He grew up in the area and loved playing in front of his friends and family. In 1999, he hit .310—his best batting average ever. Twice with the Rays, he drove in more than 100 runs.

ROBERTO HERNANDEZ   Pitcher

• BORN: 11/11/1964   • PLAYED FOR TEAM: 1998 TO 2000

Roberto Hernandez was one of the finest relief pitchers in baseball when he arrived in Tampa Bay. He showed why in the Rays' second season. Hernandez **saved** 43 of the team's 69 wins that year.

TOBY HALL   Catcher

- BORN: 10/21/1975   • PLAYED FOR TEAM: 2000 TO 2006

Toby Hall was a good hitter and a solid defensive catcher. The Tampa Bay fans loved him for his hard play—and also for the "soul patch" on his chin. Hall would dye the tuft of hair different colors to mark different occasions.

AUBREY HUFF   Infielder/Outfielder/Designated Hitter

- BORN: 12/20/1976
- PLAYED FOR TEAM: 2000 TO 2006

The Rays drafted Aubrey Huff in 1998, and he soon became Tampa Bay's most dangerous power hitter. In his career with the team, Huff hit 128 homers and had two seasons with more than 100 **runs batted in (RBIs)**.

CARL CRAWFORD   Outfielder

- BORN: 8/5/1981
- PLAYED FOR TEAM: 2002 TO 2010

Carl Crawford could have been a basketball guard or football quarterback. In fact, he turned down offers in both sports when he agreed to play for the Rays. Crawford quickly became the team's most exciting player. He led the league in triples and stolen bases four times with Tampa Bay.

LEFT: Roberto Hernandez   **ABOVE**: Aubrey Huff

B.J. UPTON   Outfielder

• BORN: 8/21/1984   • FIRST YEAR WITH TEAM: 2004

The Rays expected B.J. Upton to be their shortstop of the future. In 2007, they moved him to center field, and he became a star at his new position. He stole his 200th base for the Rays in 2011.

JAMES SHIELDS   Pitcher

• BORN: 12/20/1981   • FIRST YEAR WITH TEAM: 2006

James Shields could overpower batters with his fastball or fool them with his **change-up**. In 2011, he struck out 225 hitters and led the AL in **complete games** and **shutouts**. Shields got the nickname "Big Game James" for his ability to pitch under pressure.

BEN ZOBRIST   Second Baseman/Outfielder

• BORN: 5/26/1981

• FIRST YEAR WITH TEAM: 2006

When Ben Zobrist joined the Rays, he filled in at many different positions. In 2009, he played everywhere except pitcher and catcher. Along the way, Zobrist batted .297 with 27 homers. In 2011, he led the team in hits, runs, and doubles.

DAVID PRICE   Pitcher

- BORN: 8/26/1985
- FIRST YEAR WITH TEAM: 2008

David Price came up from the minor leagues at the end of 2008—just in time to pitch in the playoffs and World Series. He quickly became one of the top left-handed pitchers in baseball. In 2010, Price was the starter for the AL in the All-Star Game.

EVAN LONGORIA   Third Baseman

- BORN: 10/7/1985
- FIRST YEAR WITH TEAM: 2008

Evan Longoria played like an All-Star from his first day in the big leagues. He was named Rookie of the Year in 2008. A year later, he was awarded his first **Gold Glove**. Longoria always did his best when the pressure was its most intense.

DESMOND JENNINGS   Outfielder

- BORN: 10/30/1986   • FIRST YEAR WITH TEAM: 2010

The Rays love players with power and speed. Desmond Jennings gave the team both. As a rookie in 2011, he hit 10 homers and stole 20 bases after spending most of the year in the minors.

LEFT: Ben Zobrist   **ABOVE**: David Price

CALLING THE SHOTS

When a baseball team is new, it's a good idea to hire a manager and coaches who have spent a lot of years in the game. The Rays have always believed this is true. An experienced leader may not be able to turn defeat into victory. However, he can help his players form a winning attitude and pride in a job well done.

Tampa Bay's first manager was Larry Rothschild. During the 1990s, he had helped the Cincinnati Reds and Florida Marlins win championships. Rothschild was very patient with the Rays' young players. Hal McRae and Lou Piniella followed Rothschild. Both were known for being extremely competitive as players. When they managed the Rays, they asked their teams to play the same way.

In 2006, the Rays hired Joe Maddon to lead the team. He was a perfect choice. Maddon had

spent more than 30 years coaching in the majors and the minors. He worked endless hours with Tampa Bay's young stars and showed them the secrets to playing winning baseball. Maddon became famous with baseball fans for his thick black glasses and the hoodies he liked to wear on cold nights.

Maddon was like a father to many of the Tampa Bay players. He told them how proud he was when they did well. When they made mistakes, Maddon stayed calm and relaxed. He believed the life of a baseball player should be fun. Tampa Bay reached the playoffs three times during a four-year stretch under Maddon and won the pennant in 2008.

LEFT: Lou Piniella talks things over with an umpire.
ABOVE: Joe Maddon gives one of his players a fatherly smile.

ONE GREAT DAY

Tampa Bay fans were hoping that the final month of the 2011 season would be a September to remember. Unfortunately, it did not look that way early on. The New York Yankees were far ahead in the AL East. The Boston Red Sox appeared to be a sure bet to win the **Wild Card**. In order to catch Boston, the Rays had to make up nine games in less than a month.

Baseball can be a funny game. As the season drew to a close, the Red Sox simply could not win. The Rays, meanwhile, couldn't seem to lose. They closed the gap on Boston with four victories in a row. On the final day of the season, Tampa Bay had a chance to pass the Red Sox. The Rays needed a victory, and Boston had to lose.

Things did not begin well that evening. The Red Sox took a lead against the Orioles in Baltimore. In Tampa, the Rays fell behind the Yankees 7–0. Suddenly, the Rays came alive. Evan Longoria hit a three-run homer, and Tampa Bay scored six runs in the

Evan Longoria disappears into a sea of Rays after his 12th-inning homer.

eighth inning to make it 7–6. While this was happening, the Orioles were turning the tables on the Red Sox.

In the ninth inning in Tampa, the Yankees got two quick outs. The Rays sent Dan Johnson to bat. Johnson was hitting just .108, but he was the only player left that manager Joe Maddon could use. Johnson lined a ball down the right field line. The fans at Tropicana Stadium held their breath. The ball stayed fair and cleared the fence—the Rays had tied the game!

In the 12th inning, Longoria belted a ball toward the left field corner. It skipped off the top of the fence and into the seats for a game-winning home run. Meanwhile, the Orioles finished off their comeback with a 4–3 victory over Boston. The Rays had done what the experts thought was impossible. They had captured the AL Wild Card. It was the greatest comeback in team history.

"It was a crazy night," said Maddon afterward. "What happened out there goes beyond the imagination."

LEGEND HAS IT

WHICH RECORD-SMASHING RAY STARTED THE 2007 SEASON WITHOUT A SPOT ON THE TEAM?

LEGEND HAS IT that Carlos Pena did. At the end of spring training in 2007, the Rays told Pena that he was not playing well enough to make the club. He would have to go to the minor leagues. A last-minute injury to another player gave him a second chance—and he made the most of it. Pena won the starting job at first base and set team records for home runs, RBIs, and walks.

ABOVE: Carlos Pena
RIGHT: At 6′ 9″ Jeff Niemann barely fits on his own rookie card.

WHO WAS THE TEAM'S ALL-TIME HOMETOWN HERO?

LEGEND HAS IT that Doug Waechter was. Waechter was a pitcher who grew up right in St. Petersburg. His friends and family were thrilled when he was drafted and signed by the team in 1999. Imagine how happy they were when Waechter started his first game for Tampa Bay in 2003—and gave up two hits and no runs in nine innings to the Seattle Mariners. Waechter was just the ninth AL pitcher since 1970 to throw a shutout in his first big-league start.

WHICH RAY ONCE LOST A BATTLE WITH A BASKETBALL STAR?

LEGEND HAS IT that Jeff Niemann did. At 6′ 9″, Niemann was one of the tallest players in the majors. As a teenager in Houston, he wanted to play for the Lanier Middle School basketball team. In almost any other school at any other time, he would have been the starting center. Unfortunately for Niemann, the player he had to beat out was Emeka Okafor. Okafor went on to lead his college team to a national championship.

During the 1980s, Jim Morris tried to make it to the big leagues as a pitcher. He played in the minor leagues for several seasons, but arm injuries kept him from achieving his dream. Morris finally became discouraged. He decided to teach science at Reagan County High School near his home in Texas. He also coached the school's baseball team.

During one season in the late 1990s, Morris made a deal with his players. He promised he would give big-league baseball one more try if Reagan won the district championship. When the Owls took the title, Morris held up his end of the bargain and asked the Rays for a tryout. At first the team

LEFT: Jim Morris fires a pitch for the Rays.
RIGHT: Dennis Quaid and Morris show off their ESPY Award.

refused. Morris was 35 and had not pitched in many years. Then he threw 12 pitches at 98 miles per hour. Morris was as amazed as the Rays were. His arm had completely healed!

Tampa Bay signed Morris to a contract and sent him to the minor leagues. He pitched so well that the Rays added him to their roster in September of 1999. Morris entered a game against the Texas Rangers and struck out the first batter he faced. He pitched in 21 games for Tampa Bay in 1999 and 2000 before his old arm problems returned.

Morris retired from baseball in 2001. One year later, a movie of his life was made. *The Rookie* starred Dennis Quaid as Morris. The movie was very popular and even won an ESPY Award as the top sports movie of the year in 2002.

TEAM SPIRIT

When a baseball team becomes successful, a lot of new fans "jump on the bandwagon." In other words, people like to root for a winner. This happened in Tampa Bay during the 2008 season, and the Rays have remained one of baseball's more popular teams.

At a Rays game, fans have lots of ways to enjoy themselves. They can sit in regular seats or watch games from special party areas in the outfield. There is a place to have your own baseball card made and another where kids can play carnival games. Just behind the center field fence, a large tank is home to more than 30 cownose rays. Fans can touch and feed them throughout the game. The tank was created with help from the Florida Aquarium in Tampa.

LEFT: Toby Hall signs autographs for Rays fans.
ABOVE: Many fans bought this pennant after the Rays changed their team colors and logo in 2008.

TIMELINE

Greg Vaughn

1998
The Rays play their first season.

2000
Greg Vaughn leads the team with 28 homers.

1995
Baseball owners vote to add the Rays to the AL.

1999
Wade Boggs slams a home run for the 3,000th hit of his career.

Wade Boggs swings for his 3,000th hit in 1999.

James
Shields

2008
The Rays play in their first World Series.

2011
James Shields sets a team record with four shutouts.

2003
Rocco Baldelli leads all rookies with 184 hits.

2007
Carl Crawford blasts a home run in the All-Star Game.

2010
The Rays win their second AL East crown.

Rocco
Baldelli

FUN FACTS

PERFECT 10

In the second game of a doubleheader in 2008, Ben Zobrist set a team record with eight RBIs. He had already driven in two runs in the first game, giving him 10 for the day.

THAT'S A NO-NO

In high school, Scott Kazmir pitched four no-hitters in a row. He missed a fifth by one out—and then pitched no-hitters in his next two games!

STORMY WEATHER

In September of 2000, a game was postponed at Tropicana Field because of bad weather. It was just the third time that had ever happened at a domed baseball stadium.

ABOVE: Scott Kazmir   **RIGHT**: Akinori Iwamura

MR. 200

During his years with the Rays, Fred McGriff became the second player ever to hit 200 homers in the AL and NL. The first player was Frank Robinson, a member of the Hall of Fame.

ONE OF A KIND

On August 7, 1999, Wade Boggs launched a home run against the Cleveland Indians for the 3,000th hit of his career. Before Boggs, 22 other players had reached this mark. But he was the first player to do so with a homer.

HAVE GLOVE, WILL TRAVEL

When Japanese star Akinori Iwamura signed with the Rays in 2007, he was not sure which position he would play for the team. Iwamura played it safe—he brought five different gloves to his first practice.

FAMILY GAME

Andy Sonnanstine's great uncle is Ken Keltner, who was an All-Star in the 1940s. He was famous for stopping Joe DiMaggio's 56-game hitting streak with two great fielding plays.

TALKING BASEBALL

"It's all been a dream come true."
▶ *EVAN LONGORIA*, ON BECOMING A BIG LEAGUER
AND PLAYING FOR THE RAYS

"I'm ready to win. That's
what I think about. I
just want to find a way
to win."
▶ *CARL CRAWFORD*, ON
STAYING FOCUSED ALL
SEASON LONG

"I love playing baseball. I love being around baseball."
▶ *DAVID PRICE*, ON THE THRILL OF PLAYING IN THE MAJORS

"I always had power. For me, it was just a matter of
making contact."
▶ *FRED McGRIFF*, ON LEARNING TO HIT
HOME RUNS IN THE BIG LEAGUES

"I enjoy the game. It's a great game, and I enjoy being around the players and teaching and watching them get better."

▶ **JOE MADDON**, *ON THE FUN OF BEING A MANAGER*

"It's amazing what can happen when you put a bunch of athletes on the field and start to believe."

▶ **CLIFF FLOYD**, *ON THE RAYS' 2008 AL CHAMPIONSHIP*

"I tried to be as normal and calm as possible."

▶ **MATT MOORE**, *ON PITCHING IN THE PLAYOFFS AS A ROOKIE*

LEFT: Carl Crawford   **ABOVE**: Joe Maddon

GREAT DEBATES

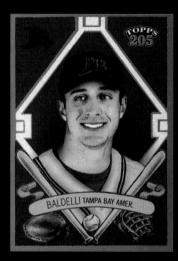

eople who root for the Rays love to compare their favorite moments, teams, and players. Some debates have been going on for years! How would you settle these classic baseball arguments?

ROCCO BALDELLI GOT THE MOST IMPORTANT HIT IN TEAM HISTORY …

… because it gave the Rays the run they needed to win the pennant in 2008. It came in the fifth inning of Game 7 of the ALCS. The score was knotted 1–1. Baldelli (LEFT) smashed a hard grounder into left field. Willie Aybar rounded third and slid home to break the tie. The Rays held on to win 3–1.

NOTHING TOPS DAN JOHNSON'S HOMER IN THE FINAL GAME OF THE 2011 SEASON …

… because the Rays were down to their last strike and needed a win to have a chance at the playoffs. Tampa Bay trailed by a run with two outs in the bottom of the ninth. Johnson was having a tough season, but his teammates had confidence in him, even if many fans thought the year was over. Johnson crushed a pitch that bounced off the foul pole for a home run to keep the season alive.

... because he gave the team a big bat in the middle of the lineup. The Rays already had good pitching, speed, and defense when the season started. What they didn't have was a slugger who scared other teams. Longoria became that hitter. He was given a big responsibility, and he came through with 27 home runs. Longoria was the key to Tampa Bay's AL championship.

JASON BARTLETT WAS ACTUALLY THE MISSING PIECE IN THE RAYS' PUZZLE THAT SEASON ...

... because sometimes the statistics don't tell you the whole story. Bartlett (RIGHT) came to the Rays in a trade and was soon the team's most dependable player. He was a talented hitter and fielder who never let his teammates down. Bartlett batted ninth most of the year, but he was really like a second **leadoff hitter**. Time and again, he either started

a big inning for the Rays or kept one going. At the end of the season, the local sportswriters voted him team MVP.

The great Rays teams and players have left their marks on the record books. These are the "best of the best" …

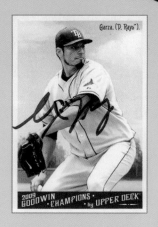

RAYS AWARD WINNERS

WINNER	AWARD	YEAR
Carlos Pena	Comeback Player of the Year	2007
Evan Longoria	Rookie of the Year	2008
Joe Maddon	Manager of the Year	2008
Matt Garza	ALCS MVP	2008
Carl Crawford	All-Star Game MVP	2009
Jeremy Hellickson	Rookie of the Year	2011
Joe Maddon	Manager of the Year	2011

ABOVE: Matt Garza was the star of the 2008 ALCS.
RIGHT: Evan Longoria takes a big swing.

RAYS ACHIEVEMENTS

ACHIEVEMENT	YEAR
AL East Champs	2008
AL Pennant Winner	2008
AL East Champs	2010
AL Wild Card Winner	2011

TOP RIGHT: Desmond Jennings helped the Rays win the 2011 Wild Card.
BOTTOM RIGHT: Carlos Pena hit 46 home runs in 2007.
BELOW: Dioner Navarro tags out a runner in 2008.

PINPOINTS

The history of a baseball team is made up of many smaller stories. These stories take place all over the map—not just in the city a team calls "home." Match the pushpins on these maps to the **TEAM FACTS**, and you will begin to see the story of the Rays unfold!

TEAM FACTS

1 St. Petersburg, Florida—*The team has played here since 1998.*

2 Philadelphia, Pennsylvania—*The Rays played in the 2008 World Series here.*

3 Norfolk, Virginia—*B.J. Upton was born here.*

4 New York, New York—*Carl Crawford won the 2008 All-Star Game MVP here.*

5 Marion, Ohio—*Aubrey Huff was born here.*

6 Omaha, Nebraska—*Wade Boggs was born here.*

7 Houston, Texas—*Scott Kazmir was born here.*

8 Petaluma, California—*Jonny Gomes was born here.*

9 Tacoma, Washington—*Toby Hall was born here.*

10 Havana, Cuba—*Rolando Arrojo was born here.*

11 Santurce, Puerto Rico—*Roberto Hernandez was born here.*

12 Ehime, Japan—*Akinori Iwamura was born here.*

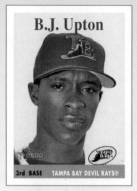

B.J. Upton

GLOSSARY

🔊 **AL EAST**—A group of American League teams that play in the eastern part of the country.

🔊 **ALL-STAR GAME**—Baseball's annual game featuring the best players from the American League and National League.

🔊 **AMERICAN LEAGUE (AL)**—One of baseball's two major leagues; the AL began play in 1901.

🔊 **AMERICAN LEAGUE CHAMPIONSHIP SERIES (ALCS)**—The playoff series that has decided the American League pennant since 1969.

🔊 **CHANGE-UP**—A slow pitch disguised to look like a fastball.

🔊 **CLUTCH**—Pressure situations.

🔊 **COMPLETE GAMES**—Games started and finished by the same pitcher.

🧠 *CONTENDER*—A person, group, or team that competes for a championship.

🧠 *DECISIVE*—Final.

🔊 **DRAFT**—The annual meeting at which teams take turns choosing the best players in high school and college.

🔊 **GOLD GLOVE**—The award given each year to baseball's best fielders.

🔊 **LEADOFF HITTER**—The first hitter in a lineup, or the first hitter in an inning.

🧠 *LOGO*—A symbol or design that represents a company or team.

🔊 **MINOR LEAGUES**—The many professional leagues that help develop players for the major leagues.

🔊 **NATIONAL LEAGUE (NL)**—The older of the two major leagues; the NL began play in 1876.

🔊 **PENNANT**—A league championship. The term comes from the triangular flag awarded to each season's champion, beginning in the 1870s.

🔊 **PLAYOFFS**—The games played after the regular season to determine which teams will advance to the World Series.

🔊 **POSTSEASON**—The games played after the regular season, including the playoffs and World Series.

🧠 *REMODELED*—Changed or improved.

🔊 **RUNS BATTED IN (RBIs)**—A statistic that counts the number of runners a batter drives home.

🔊 **SAVED**—Recorded the last out or outs in a team's win. A relief pitcher on the mound at the end of a close victory is credited with a "save."

🔊 **SHUTOUTS**—Games in which one team does not score a run.

🧠 *VETERANS*—Players with great experience.

🔊 **WILD CARD**—A playoff spot reserved for a team that does not win its division, but finishes with a good record.

🔊 **WORLD SERIES**—The world championship series played between the AL and NL pennant winners.

EXTRA INNINGS

TEAM SPIRIT introduces a great way to stay up to date with your team! Visit our **EXTRA INNINGS** link and get connected to the latest and greatest updates. **EXTRA INNINGS** serves as a young reader's ticket to an exclusive web page—with more stories, fun facts, team records, and photos of the Rays. Content is updated during and after each season. The **EXTRA INNINGS** feature also enables readers to send comments and letters to the author! Log onto:

www.norwoodhousepress.com/library.aspx

and click on the tab: **TEAM SPIRIT** to access **EXTRA INNINGS**.

Read all the books in the series to learn more about professional sports. For a complete listing of the baseball, basketball, football, and hockey teams in the **TEAM SPIRIT** series, visit our website at:

www.norwoodhousepress.com/library.aspx

ON THE ROAD

TAMPA BAY RAYS
One Tropicana Drive
St. Petersburg, Florida 33705
(727) 825-3137
tampabay.rays.mlb.com

NATIONAL BASEBALL HALL OF FAME AND MUSEUM
25 Main Street
Cooperstown, New York 13326
(888) 425-5633
www.baseballhalloffame.org

ON THE BOOKSHELF

To learn more about the sport of baseball, look for these books at your library or bookstore:

* Augustyn, Adam (editor). *The Britannica Guide to Baseball*. New York, NY: Rosen Publishing, 2011.

* Dreier, David. *Baseball: How It Works*. North Mankato, MN: Capstone Press, 2010.

* Stewart, Mark. *Ultimate 10: Baseball*. New York, NY: Gareth Stevens Publishing, 2009.

INDEX

PAGE NUMBERS IN **BOLD** REFER TO ILLUSTRATIONS.

ABOUT THE AUTHOR

MARK STEWART has written more than 50 books on baseball and over 150 sports books for kids. He grew up in New York City during the 1960s rooting for the Yankees and Mets, and was lucky enough to meet players from both teams. Mark comes from a family of writers. His grandfather was Sunday Editor of *The New York Times,* and his mother was Articles Editor of *Ladies' Home Journal* and *McCall's.* Mark has profiled hundreds of athletes over the past 25 years. He has also written several books about his native New York and New Jersey, his home today. Mark is a graduate of Duke University, with a degree in history. He lives and works in a home overlooking Sandy Hook, New Jersey. You can contact Mark through the Norwood House Press website.